# Truant

presents the world premi~

# The Right Ballerina
By Billy Cowan

**Playdead Press**

**Published by Playdead Press 2012**

© Billy Cowan 2012

Billy Cowan has asserted his rights under the
Copyright, Design and Patents Act, 1988, to be
identified as the author of this work.

A CIP catalogue record for this book is available from
the British Library.

ISBN 978-0-9572859-8-9

**Playdead Press**
**www.playdeadpress.com**

*The Right Ballerina* was first performed at The Lowry Studio, Salford on 12th October 2012.  The cast was as follows:

| | |
|---|---|
| Penny | Helen MacFarlane |
| Jack | Adam Grayson |
| Trevor | Steve Moorewood |
| Mr X | Richard Sails |

| | |
|---|---|
| Director | Billy Cowan |
| Designer | Colin Eccleston |
| Sound/Music | Jamie Summers |
| Choreographer | Julia Griffin |
| Stage Manager | Joe Colgan |

*The Right Ballerina* is produced by Truant Company with the generous support of Arts Council England and The National Lottery.

Truant would like to thank the following people and organisations who have helped in the journey towards production:

Arts Council England; M6 Theatre Company; Chris Honer, Artistic Director of The Library Theatre Manchester; Chris Bridgman of North West Playwrights; Salford University and Lisa Moore; Punam Ramchurn, Oldham Council Literature Officer; Gary Everett, Artistic Director of Homotopia; Simon Bent and Manchester Salon; The Peggy Ramsay Foundation; Stenaline; Penny McDonald; Rowan Davies.

## Adam Grayson as Jack

Adam began his career as a member of the Bolton Octagon Youth Theatre (Activ8).

There he played Danny in *The Year My Voice Broke* adapted by Peter Kay. He then went on to study acting at the Royal Academy of Dramatic Art. During training he wrote a play, *Quids & Dimps* which won the Royal Exchange's WRITE 02 competition and was performed in their studio. Recently he's played Jane Austen's romantic heroes Mr Darcy & Mr Knightley. He has also played Petruchio in *The Taming of the Shrew* and Antonio in *The Merchant of Venice*. Adam is delighted to undertake this unique role of Jack Stevens.


## Helen MacFarlane as Penny

Helen graduated from RSAMD in July 2011. Theatre credits include: Young Woman in *Knives in Hens* - Theatre by the Lake, Keswick; Carrie in *The Nutcracker Prince* and Edith in *Blithe Spirit* - Stephen Joseph Theatre, Scarborough; Ella in *Loaded* - 24:7 Theatre Festival, Manchester; and Mary Warren in *The Crucible* - York Theatre Royal. Training credits include Queen Elizabeth in *Richard III* and Chorus in the RSC *Sneak Preview Event* to open the newly refurbished Royal Shakespeare Theatre, Stratford Upon Avon.

## Richard Sails as Mr X

Richard trained at Arden Theatre School, Manchester. Credits include:
*Deck The Hall, Richard III, Much Ado About Nothing,* Demi-Paradise Productions; *Contrecoup,* Second Nature; *Rosencrantz And Guildenstern Are Dead,* Manchester Library Theatre; *Richard III,* Trickster Theatre; *Plus One* and *Full House,* MediaMedea; *Of Mice And Men* and *The Tempest,* Black Box Theatre; Dr Watson in *The Hound Of The Baskervilles,* Gawsworth Hall; *Heart Is A Lonely Hunter,* Truant Company; *Toxing It,* Meant-2-Play Productions; *Beauty & The Beast,* Mad About Productions; *Dev's Army,* Elysion Productions; *Look Back In Anger,* Blackhand Productions. TV includes *Coronation Street, Hollyoaks, In The City* and *Emmerdale.*

## Steve Moorewood as Trevor

Steve started out as an actor and writer in children's theatre before moving into children's television. He spent six wonderful years at *The Children's Channel* where he wrote and performed in countless sketches, sit-coms and game shows. Since then he's played in Shakespeare, drama and farce and loves to put on his heels and strut his stuff as a pantomime dame. Steve's TV roles have been equally varied – he's crashed an aeroplane on *999*

*Lifesavers*, worked alongside screen legends Tony Curtis and Mr Blobby on *Noel's House Party* and, most recently, made his third appearance in *Emmerdale*.

## Billy Cowan – Writer/Director

Billy has an MPhil(B) in Playwriting from Birmingham University. He is an award-winning playwright having won the 2002 Writing Out Award for Best New Gay Play organised by Finborough Theatre, London for his play *Smilin' Through*. He also won Warehouse Theatre's 2010 International Playwriting award for *Transitions*. His plays include *Care Takers, Stigmata, Smilin' Through* (nominated for Best New Play 2005 by the Manchester Evening News), and *Heart is a Lonely Hunter*. He has also written for young audiences: *Sidelined* and *Straight Talk* for Bolton Octagon Activ8 group and *Web Pal* and *It Should Have Been Me* for M6 Theatre Company.

## Julia Griffin – choreographer

Julia is a dance artist working in the UK and Europe with extensive experience in teaching, performing and choreographing contemporary dance and dance video/film works. She has worked collaboratively on small to large-scale projects with visual artists, musicians, photographers, video and sound artists, leading choreographers and film directors. Collaborations include: Emilyn Claid, David Massingham, Igloo, Black Grape, Siobhan Davies, Penny Arcade, Wendy Houston, Julie Tollentino, Katherine Dawson, Beautiful South, and Rachel Davies. She worked with Marina Abramovic on *Luminosity* and Joan Jonas on *Mirror Check*, which was part of Manchester International Festival 2011. www.griffindance.tk

## Colin Eccleston - Designer

Colin graduated from Liverpool Institute of Performing Arts in 2011 where he developed his passion for theatre design and puppetry. After graduating he reached the final of The Linbury prize (The UK's most prestigious prize for upcoming theatre designers) and his work was displayed in the National Theatre. He has been a designer on several shows including Spike Theatre's award winning *The Games* and Lip Service Theatre's *Inspector Norse*. He has also taught Puppetry mechanics as visiting lecturer at LIPA and has recently devised a roaming puppet show that premiered in Portmeirion's *Festival No.6*.

## Joe Colgan – Stage Manager/Technical

Joe Colgan is a freelance Stage and Production Manager based in the North West. He has worked on a variety of comedic, dramatic and musical projects for theatre, film and television across the UK. As well as touring productions, he has worked extensively for arts and fringe festivals. With experience in Lighting and Sound, recent projects have included designs for performances at The Lowry Theatre and Royal Northern College of Music.

## Jamie Summers – Music

Summers is a Jamie of all trades. He lives and works in Manchester as an artist and is a regular collaborator with Truant Company having created animation for their multimedia monologue *Daddy* at Birmingham Repertory Theatre and music for *Care Takers*. He also designed the set for *Stigmata* as well as making a shrine to Susan Sarandon. He designs all of Truant's marketing materials as well as their website. Primarily he is a visual artist and his paintings, drawings and screenprints can be seen at www.jamiesummers.co.uk

**Truant Company** is director Natalie Wilson and writer Billy Cowan. They met in 2003 when Natalie directed a rehearsed reading of Billy's 2002 Writing Out International award-winning script *Smilin' Through* - a competition launched by The Finborough Theatre, London looking for new gay or lesbian plays.

Sharing the same dream of developing and producing new queer specific work, they joined forces and launched Truant Company in May 2004. Their first piece of work was a multimedia monologue for Birmingham Rep called *Daddy* in 2004, followed by *Heart Is A Lonely Hunter* at Manchester's 24:7 Festival. Right from the start Truant's work made an impact with Giles Haworth in his **A Year in Theatre, Greater Manchester** describing Heart as "possibly the most interesting play in the festival" and that Truant was "a very significant addition to Manchester's theatrical resources."

Heart Is A Lonely Hunter was then followed in 2005 with a co-production of *Smilin' Through* with Birmingham Rep, Contact in Manchester and Queer Up North. The play was nominated for Best New Play of the year by The Manchester Evening News and was remounted by The Drill Hall in London in 2007.

Other works include **Stigmata** (2006) which was produced by The Drill Hall and directed by Natalie. In 2009 Billy wrote and directed a new play called **Care Takers** which toured to the Dublin Gay Theatre Festival, An Tain in Dundalk, The Lowry, The Unity in Liverpool as part of Homotopia and The Oldham Coliseum. The play was selected by The Library Theatre, Manchester as one of the best studio plays of the year and was remounted in 2010 for their Re:Play Festival.

During this time both Natalie and Billy have pursued individual careers as well as keeping Truant together. Natalie is now Artistic Director of Theatre Centre in London and Billy manages M6 Theatre Company's participation department as well as teaching playwriting at Edge Hill University.

# The Right Ballerina

by
Billy Cowan

*For Jamie and Reb*

<u>Characters</u>

PENNY, *thirty*

JACK, *forties*

Mr X, *fifties*

TREVOR, *forties*

JOURNALIST 1
JOURNALIST 2

*The play is set in the Artistic Director's office of a leading dance company.*

*( / ) indicates the point when the following speech interrupts.*

*A name without a line of dialogue indicates when that character chooses not to speak or is unsure of what to say.*

*The play is best performed without an interval. However, if an interval is desired it should come at the end of Scene Nine.*

*The play can be performed with or without dance. It is up to the director to decide where the dance elements should take place. In this first production Penny dances at the beginning of the play, before Scene One commences, and then at the end of the play.*

# ONE

*Office. We hear whistles and chants from outside. Jack, the Artistic Director, is moving around some furniture trying to find a new lay-out that he likes. He takes a large framed picture of Giselle off the wall and tries to see if it will look good on another wall. He goes to the phone.*

JACK          Taz, can you ring marketing darling? Ask them to bring up a selection of posters from last season. Thanks dear.

*He goes back to rearranging the furniture. Trevor enters and goes straight to the window.*

TREVOR     They're fucking still out there.

JACK          Good morning, Trevor.

TREVOR     Haven't they got jobs to go to, for fuck sake.

JACK          Oh good morning Jack and how are you this morning?

TREVOR     I'm glad you're finding this amusing.

JACK          Relax Trevor. I'd rather not have to deal with another one of your heart attacks.

TREVOR     Where are these people coming from for Christ's sake?

JACK          Blame Marc Zuckerberg.

TREVOR     Who?

JACK          Never mind.

TREVOR     Have you spoken to Penny yet?

3

| | |
|---|---|
| JACK | I'm expecting her any minute. |
| TREVOR | If it's true, what are we going to do? |
| JACK | Nothing. |
| TREVOR | Nothing. What do you mean, nothing? |
| JACK | I don't think there's anything we can do. |
| TREVOR | I want this sorted, Jack. The Board want it sorted. |
| JACK | It'll blow over in a few days, just wait and see. |
| TREVOR | If it's true, she'll have to go. We'll have to get rid of her. |
| JACK | That's a bit overdramatic. |
| TREVOR | She's getting on a bit now anyway. I mean, how old is she? Thirty? She can't have many years left and to be perfectly frank, it shows. |
| JACK | She's still the best dancer we've got. |
| TREVOR | We'll find someone else. |
| JACK | She'd have us for unfair dismissal. |
| TREVOR | Something needs to be done, dear boy. Those lot with their little banners and fucking whistles want us to get rid of her. |
| JACK | They haven't said that. All they've said is they want to meet with us. |
| TREVOR | It's obvious what they want. |
| JACK | Let's just wait and see, shall we? We don't even know if it's true yet. |
| TREVOR | Don't we? |
| JACK | What's that supposed to mean? |

4

| | |
|---|---|
| TREVOR | You were in a relationship with her, dear boy. You must know what foot she kicks with. |
| JACK | Do you know everything about your friends? |
| TREVOR | I know who Jason votes for. |
| JACK | We were only together a year, Trevor. |
| TREVOR | Yes, but you've known each other a long time. |
| JACK | You've known me a long time. Do you think I'd lie about a thing like this? |

*Pause.*

| | |
|---|---|
| TREVOR | Of course not, dear boy. But people are talking. Some of the Board... well, you know what they're like. |
| JACK | Look, I'd be very much surprised if it were true, so let's just see what happens. I'm sure it's all a storm in a teacup. We'll just have to ride it out. |
| TREVOR | The Board's arses aren't hard enough to ride it out. Especially if box office keeps falling. |
| JACK | They've only been protesting a few days, Trevor. The fall in box office can't be attributed to that. |
| TREVOR | It's down thirty-two percent from last week. What other reason could there be? |

5

JACK        We're going through a recession if you
            haven't noticed.

TREVOR      The upper middle-classes don't have
            recessions Jack, you know that.

JACK        Well maybe it's the weather. There could
            be any number of explanations, so let's not
            jump to conclusions.

TREVOR      Whatever the reason, Jack, the Board
            wants it sorted out as quickly as possible.
            And with minimum damage to our profile.

JACK        It goes without saying.

TREVOR      Well don't let me down.

JACK        Have I ever?

*Trevor looks out the window.*

TREVOR      Self-righteous twats.

*The door knocks.*

JACK        That'll be Penny. Come in.

*Penny enters.*

TREVOR      Penny, darling.

*He goes over to her and kisses her on the cheek.*

TREVOR      You look fabulous. Doesn't she look
            fabulous, Jack?

| | |
|---|---|
| PENNY | Thanks Trevor. You don't look so bad yourself. |
| TREVOR | Nonsense. I'm a fat, middle-aged old poof who eats too many crème brulee's and drinks too much red wine. Anyway, I must be running along. Jason's dragging me to Selfridges to find something '*dee-lish*' for our god-daughter's birthday. I'll speak to you soon and don't let those bastards drag you down. |

*He exits. Jack and Penny stare at each other.*

| | |
|---|---|
| JACK | It's good to see you. Would you like a drink? |
| PENNY | No thanks. |
| JACK | How've you been keeping? |
| PENNY | Fine. |
| JACK | Good. |

*Pause.*

| | |
|---|---|
| PENNY | Thinking of jumping ship? |
| JACK | Oh no, darling. Just bored. Need something new to look at. How's Marion? |
| PENNY | Sick, I'm afraid. |
| JACK | Nothing serious I hope. |
| PENNY | We don't know yet. |
| JACK | I'm sure it's nothing. Will you send my regards? |

7

| | |
|---|---|
| PENNY | You could pop in and see her. Have a cup of tea. She misses you. |
| JACK | I might just do that. |
| PENNY | Just because we've split doesn't / mean |
| JACK | Yes, I know. I will. I'll pop in and see her. |
| PENNY | Good. |

*Pause.*

| | |
|---|---|
| JACK | I've missed you. |
| PENNY | Really? |
| JACK | Yes. |
| PENNY | You haven't spoken to me in three months. |
| JACK | I've been up to my eyes… you know what it's like. |
| PENNY | You didn't drop into rehearsals. |
| JACK | No / I… |
| PENNY | You always pop into rehearsals. |
| JACK | Yes. I try to. When I'm not busy. |
| PENNY | We said we wouldn't let it affect the work, Jack. |
| JACK | Yes. It won't. I'm sorry. I just thought we could do with some space. |
| PENNY | I want us to be friends. |
| JACK | So do I, darling. |
| PENNY | We have to try. |
| JACK | Of course. |
| PENNY | Good. |

*Pause.*

JACK        Penny, we need to talk about the disruptions.

PENNY       Yes, I could tell. You've got your work face on.

JACK        Work face?

PENNY       You always have it on when there's something up.

JACK        Am I that obvious?

PENNY       Botox might help.

JACK        Botox? Oh I see … yes. (*He forces a laugh.*) Yes, maybe I'll give it a go.

*Pause.*

PENNY       I forgive you, Jack.

JACK

PENNY       You know that. Don't you?

JACK        You forgive me?

PENNY       Yes.

*Pause.*

JACK        Penny look, let's talk about the disruptions.

PENNY       Yes, the disruptions.

JACK        They're becoming a problem.

PENNY       Aggravating little shits.

JACK        Yes.

9

| | |
|---|---|
| PENNY | They'll soon stop. |
| JACK | It's already affecting ticket sales. |
| PENNY | They can't keep it up. |
| JACK | Three times this week, Penny. |
| PENNY | They're nothing but a group of interfering busy bodies who've found themselves a little campaign to get all excited about. They'll soon be onto the next one. |
| JACK | You may be right darling, but we're going to have to meet with them. |
| PENNY | |
| JACK | They said the disruptions would continue until we met with them. |
| PENNY | No, Jack. |
| JACK | They've left us no choice. |
| PENNY | They'll make demands. Unreasonable demands. They'll want you to get rid of me. |
| JACK | That won't happen darling, so don't worry. |
| PENNY | Please, Jack. Don't see them. |
| JACK | We have to. |
| PENNY | Trouble-making scum. |

*Pause.*

| | |
|---|---|
| JACK | Before I meet them, Penny. I need to know if there's any truth in their accusation. |
| PENNY | |

| | |
|---|---|
| JACK | Forgive me, darling. I know it's probably a lot of stuff and nonsense but I need to ask. You understand? |
| PENNY | I'd rather not say, Jack. |
| JACK | |
| PENNY | I don't have to say. |
| JACK | Of / course not... |
| PENNY | It's private. |
| JACK | Yes. Yes it is. |
| PENNY | I can put my X in whichever box I like. Right? |
| JACK | Yes... |
| PENNY | It's my business no-one elses. (*Pause.*) I can't get fired, can I? |
| JACK | No. Don't be silly. |
| PENNY | Even if it's true? |
| JACK | No. |
| PENNY | That would be unethical... Undemocratic. |
| JACK | Yes, but... |
| PENNY | But... you need to know. |
| JACK | I'm afraid so. |

*Pause.*

| | |
|---|---|
| PENNY | Yes. |
| JACK | Their accusation is true? |
| PENNY | Yes. |
| JACK | Oh... I see. |

*Pause.*

| | |
|---|---|
| PENNY | Don't look at me like that, Jack. I'm not an active member. I joined when I was young. |
| JACK | Right... |
| PENNY | It's not a big part of my life. It's something I did on the spare of the moment. |
| JACK | I never knew... you never told me. |
| PENNY | But why would I? |

*Pause.*

| | |
|---|---|
| JACK | Of course. You're right. |
| PENNY | It wasn't important, Jack. It's not important. |
| JACK | |
| PENNY | You're making judgements now, aren't you? I can tell. |
| JACK | No. No, I'm just... slightly taken aback. |

*Pause.*

| | |
|---|---|
| PENNY | It's the issue of immigration I feel strongly about. |
| JACK | There's no need to explain. |
| PENNY | We're only a small island, Jack. |
| JACK | Penny / don't... |
| PENNY | It's nothing to do with race. |
| JACK | Of course / not... |
| PENNY | Then there's Europe... |

12

| | |
|---|---|
| JACK | Stop / Penny. |
| PENNY | I'm not sure it's working. |
| JACK | Penny darling, please stop. |
| PENNY | I'm entitled to my beliefs, Jack. |
| JACK | Of course you are. |
| PENNY | Then don't meet with them. |
| JACK | I have to. |
| PENNY | Do you really, Jack? |
| JACK | Afraid so. |
| PENNY | Really? |

*Jack nods.*

| | |
|---|---|
| PENNY | I've dedicated my life to this company. |
| JACK | I know. |
| PENNY | I've helped make it what it is today. |
| JACK | Don't worry, darling. |
| PENNY | But I am worried. |
| JACK | You're our principal dancer. People fly from all over the world to see you. We'll sort it out. |
| PENNY | Promise? |
| JACK | Yes. |
| PENNY | Thank you, Jack. |

*Pause.*

| | |
|---|---|
| JACK | There's just one other thing. |
| PENNY | |

| | |
|---|---|
| JACK | I've asked Christina to cover your performance. |
| PENNY | Jack... |
| JACK | It's a precaution. Just for tonight... until I can meet with them. |
| PENNY | That's not fair, Jack. |
| JACK | Don't be upset, darling. |
| PENNY | I am upset. |
| JACK | I understand, but it's for the best. |
| PENNY | The public will be disappointed. |
| JACK | I know. |
| PENNY | They come to see me. |
| JACK | We'll say you've come down with something. |
| PENNY | I've never missed a performance. Not one. |
| JACK | Just for tonight darling. I promise. |
| PENNY | Those bastards. |
| JACK | I know. But we'll soon have it sorted out. Trust me. |

*Pause.*

| | |
|---|---|
| PENNY | Can I trust you, Jack? |
| JACK | Of course. |
| PENNY | This has nothing to do with... us... the baby? |
| JACK | What do you mean? |
| PENNY | You might be looking for an excuse to get rid of me. |
| JACK | How can you think that? |

14

*Pause.*

PENNY          I'm sorry.

JACK           We've known each other a long time,
               Penny. No matter what's happened,
               you're still my little Giselle.

PENNY          Thank you, Jack.

JACK           I'll soon have it sorted. Now go home and
               tell Marion I'll call in on her in a few days
               time.

PENNY          Thanks Jack.


**TWO**

*Next day. The picture of Giselle is still on the floor leaning
against the wall. Jack is signing papers. The door knocks. He
gets up and answers it. Mr X enters carrying a satchel.*

JACK           Come in.

*Jack approaches him and holds out his hand.*

               Jack. Won't you take a seat? Would you
               like a drink of something?

MR X           A drink? Um... yes. Sorry, no. It's fine.
               I've got some... some water here...
               somewhere.

15

*He searches in his satchel.*

|        | Here it is. |
| JACK | Are you sure you wouldn't like something stronger? I've got an extremely good Scotch... one of the perks of having a major distillery as a sponsor. |
| MR X | No. Water's fine, thank you. |
| JACK | You don't mind if I...? |

*He pours himself a drink.*

| MR X | I've never been in an Artistic Director's office before. |
| JACK | It's just like any other office really. A few more pictures maybe. |
| MR X | It's very nice. Artistic... |
| JACK | Yes. |

*Jack laughs. Mr X looks confused.*

| MR X | Anyway, thank you for meeting with us so promptly. |
| JACK | Well, as you can imagine, we want to get it resolved as quickly as possible. |
| MR X | Yes. |
| JACK | Can I just say upfront that I personally sympathise with your concerns Mr... um... |
| MR X | X. |

| | |
|---|---|
| JACK | Mr X? |
| MR X | Yes. |
| JACK | Really? |
| MR X | If you need to refer to me by name, please use Mr X. |
| JACK | Are you being serious? |
| MR X | I know it sounds strange but we like things to remain objective and impersonal. We've found it works best in this type of context. |
| JACK | I see. Well, I don't see actually, but if that's what you want, then so be it. |
| MR X | It's not what I want, Mr Stevens. It's how my organisation requires it. |

*Pause.*

| | |
|---|---|
| JACK | Right... Well Mr X, let's get down to business then, shall we? |
| MR X | Please do. |
| JACK | What is it you want from us? |
| MR X | My organisation. |
| JACK | Sorry? |
| MR X | What does my organisation want? |
| JACK | Of course, that's what I meant. |
| MR X | It may seem pedantic but we must be clear on these things. I'm just a spokesperson. |
| JACK | Of course. |
| MR X | For my organisation. |
| JACK | Yes. |
| MR X | For the UK branch of my organisation. |

17

| | |
|---|---|
| JACK | Mr X, what does your organisation want? |
| MR X | Sorry. I'm holding things up. It's just that I don't want... *we* don't want any misunderstandings. Language can be very tricky you know. |
| JACK | I'm sure it can. Now please... what do you... I mean what does your organisation want? |
| MR X | Well, it has come to our attention that Ms Leigh / your principal dancer |
| JACK | I've seen the placards, Mr X. I've heard the chants. I know what your complaint is. |
| MR X | Then you should know what we require. |
| JACK | I'm not sure I do. |

*Pause.*

| | |
|---|---|
| MR X | Mr Stevens, your principal dancer belongs to a right-wing political party. |
| JACK | Yes, I know. And I'm just as shocked about it as the next person but ... well people are entitled to their views, aren't they? |
| MR X | Don't you find it despicable? |
| JACK | I can't say I'm happy about it but Ms Leigh's political beliefs are personal. We cannot interfere in personal matters. |

| | |
|---|---|
| MR X | But it's not just any right-wing political party, it's the most vile / the most dangerous |
| JACK | Yes I know and I agree. But we live in a democracy Mr X and Ms Leigh has a right to her views just like you and I have a right to ours. I don't honestly know what you expect me to do. |
| MR X | We'd like you to do what's right, Mr Stevens. |
| JACK | But there's nothing I can do. Legally there's nothing I nor the Company can do. |
| MR X | We would like you to ask her to withdraw her membership from that party and to publicly denounce them. The protests, I'm afraid, will continue until this happens. |

*Pause.*

| | |
|---|---|
| JACK | Be reasonable, Mr X. |
| MR X | Reasonable? You are this country's leading dance company... |
| JACK | Yes. |
| MR X | And Ms Leigh is a high profile member of your company... |
| JACK | Yes. |
| MR X | By not doing anything you are promoting her political beliefs. It's as simple as that. |
| JACK | Mr X, we cannot be held responsible for the personal opinions of our employees. |

*Pause.*

| | |
|---|---|
| MR X | You are a publicly funded Company, Mr Stevens. |
| JACK | I am aware of that. |
| MR X | By employing Ms Leigh you are spending public funds on the promotion of right-wing ideology. |

*Jack laughs.*

| | |
|---|---|
| JACK | Oh sorry, but that's ridiculous. |
| MR X | Ms Leigh has publicly aligned herself to a right-wing party, has she not? |
| JACK | Not publicly, no. |
| MR X | She works in the public eye. |
| JACK | Yes / but |
| MR X | It is deplorable that someone of Ms Leigh's public standing should be associated with such a party. |
| JACK | But the public was blissfully unaware of Ms Leigh's political beliefs until your organisation brought attention to them. |

*Pause.*

| | |
|---|---|
| MR X | Do you share Ms Leigh's political beliefs, Mr Stevens? |
| JACK | Of course I don't. |

MR X             Does any member of the board share her
                 views?
JACK             No. I don't know.  I doubt it very much.
MR X             Well then, surely you can see it's in your
                 company's interest to get Ms Leigh to
                 withdraw her membership and denounce
                 that party?

*Pause.*

JACK             Mr X... I hate to say this because I too
                 wish it wasn't so but... the organisation in
                 question is a legal one.
MR X             Many people in this country wish it
                 wasn't.
JACK             That doesn't change the fact they are
                 legal. And that is why our hands are tied.
                 If they were an illegal organisation then
                 maybe we could do something about it.

*Pause.*

MR X             Your Company has a commitment to
                 racial equality. (*He searches in his satchel*)
                 It says here in your... your... oh dear,
                 where is it... here it is. In your annual
                 report on page / ten. It says...
JACK             I'm well aware of what it says in our
                 Annual Report, Mr X.

21

| | |
|---|---|
| MR X | Well then I shouldn't need to explain that Ms Leigh is in breach of her contract if she contravenes your company's race equality policy. |
| JACK | Ms Leigh is not a racist. |
| MR X | Even if that were true, her membership of that organisation contravenes your company's race commitments. |

*Pause.*

JACK   Look... Mr X. In the eighties I, like many other Doctor Martin wearing teenagers, joined the Anti-Nazi League and fought against the bully boys of the National Front. At Durham University I became a member of the Socialist Workers Party and CND. I've even wore a PLO scarf and walked in support of the Miners, the Liverpool Dockers and against the war on Iraq. So I can totally sympathise with your concerns. However, the older I become the more I realise that freedom of thought and freedom of expression are the most fundamental rights we have as human beings. Therefore I cannot agree with your tactics. Ms Leigh has a right to her beliefs no matter how objectionable you or I may find them. I cannot ask her to withdraw from her party or to publicly

|         | denounce them. I hope you can understand. |
|---------|----------|
| MR X    | I see. |
| JACK    | I'm / sorry but... |
| MR X    | Our committee will not be pleased. |
| JACK    | I'm sorry, but there's really nothing I can do. |
| MR X    | Then the protests will continue. |

*He gets up to leave.*

| JACK | Mr X. Even if I ask Ms Leigh to withdraw her membership, she is under no legal obligation to do so. There is no guarantee she will do it. Can't you see that? |
|------|------|
| MR X | We must make her see it is the right thing to do, Mr Stevens. Goodbye. |

*He exits.*

**THREE**

*The following week. Jack is at his desk, Trevor sits opposite.*

| JACK | Don't go mad but... Glenmaddoch have pulled the sponsorship on the Christmas show. |
|------|------|

23

| | |
|---|---|
| TREVOR | Oh for fuck sake. We're fucked. The Board are going to go fucking ballistic. |
| JACK | I know. |
| TREVOR | The press are going to love this. Another nail in our fuckin' coffin. Great. |
| JACK | I know it's bad / but we can recover |
| TREVOR | Bad? Bad? It's a fuckin catastrophe! She's going to have to do what they want. You know that, right? |
| JACK | Yes, I know. |
| TREVOR | If she doesn't, we'll get rid of her. |
| JACK | Can we do that? Legally, I mean. |
| TREVOR | Martin thinks we can. He says it'll be difficult but... we have a case. |
| JACK | I don't want it to come to that, Trevor. She's given everything to this company. She's also made us a lot of money over the years. |
| TREVOR | But we're losing a lot of money now. |
| JACK | Yes. I know. But we owe her. |
| TREVOR | She's made a lot of money out of us too, Jack. And made a name for herself. We owe her nothing. |

*Pause.*

| | |
|---|---|
| JACK | Look. Let's not panic. We're still close. She'll listen to me. |

*Pause.*

24

| | |
|---|---|
| TREVOR | Even if she withdraws her membership, I'm not sure that'll be the end of it. Most of the Board are... unhappy to say the least. They're worried about the effect it will have on our audiences in the long run. I mean, it doesn't do us any favours to have our principal dancer associated with a racist fucking mob. Now does it? |
| JACK | She didn't know what she was doing. She was young and stupid. She doesn't understand politics. |
| TREVOR | Yes, but shit sticks Jack. People remember things. |
| JACK | Look, I've got it all worked out. I'll persuade her to withdraw her membership and then I'll help her write a statement for the press. By the time she's finished reading it, everyone will see her as the victim and those do-gooders as bully boys. I can guarantee it. |
| TREVOR | Are you sure she'll go for it? |
| JACK | Don't worry. I know how to play Penny. |

*Pause.*

| | |
|---|---|
| TREVOR | The Board doesn't want her to set foot on stage until it's all cleared up. |
| JACK | I've already scheduled Christina to cover all her performances until it's sorted. |
| TREVOR | Good. How did she take it? |

| JACK | I haven't told her yet. |
| TREVOR | Oh... rather you than me, dear boy. |
| JACK | I'll get Taz to do it. |

*They smile.*

| TREVOR | Coward. |

*Trevor exits.*


## FOUR

*Jack is writing at his desk. Penny enters.*

| JACK | Penny. Sit / down darling. |
| PENNY | No I won't sit. |
| JACK | / Please |
| PENNY | You cancel all my performances without a word... |
| JACK | I'm / sorry |
| PENNY | Not one word... |
| JACK | I / know |
| PENNY | Just bloody messages... |
| JACK | I'm / sorry |
| PENNY | Left by Taz... Do you know how that makes me feel? |
| JACK | Yes. |

| | |
|---|---|
| PENNY | Not knowing what's going on... thinking the worst... unable to speak to you. |
| JACK | I was seeking advice. |
| PENNY | You could have told me that. |
| JACK | I know. |
| PENNY | You could have called and told me. |
| JACK | Yes. |
| PENNY | You should have told me. |
| JACK | I know. |
| PENNY | You said we were still friends. |
| JACK | We are. |
| PENNY | Then I deserved better. |
| JACK | I needed to know our options Penny. To be clear before speaking to you. |
| PENNY | When can I dance again? |
| JACK | |
| PENNY | Jack? |

*Pause.*

| | |
|---|---|
| JACK | The disruptions Penny... we can't let them continue. It's got out of hand. |
| PENNY | But we can't give in to blackmail... that's what this is. |
| JACK | People aren't coming to see the show anymore. They're coming to see the disruptions. They're coming to see you humiliated... if they're coming at all. |
| PENNY | That's not true. |
| JACK | I think it is, darling. |

27

| | |
|---|---|
| PENNY | People have been supporting me. |
| JACK | Some people. |
| PENNY | People have stood up and shouted the protesters down. |
| JACK | That doesn't help. |
| PENNY | Decent people don't want them to win. They come to show them that. |
| JACK | It's become a slagging match. No-one cares about the dance anymore. |
| PENNY | Decent people care. I've had over a thousand emails supporting me, telling me how disgusted they are at the whole rotten business. |
| JACK | And I've had just as many emails demanding we get rid of you. |

*Pause.*

| | |
|---|---|
| PENNY | But read the papers Jack. |
| JACK | I have. |
| PENNY | People think it's disgusting. They believe arts and politics should be kept separate. It's my abilities as a dancer that's important. |
| JACK | It depends on which papers you read. |

*Pause.*

| | |
|---|---|
| PENNY | Whose side are you on? |
| JACK | Yours. |

28

| | |
|---|---|
| PENNY | Are you? Are you really? |
| JACK | I'm on your side Penny but I'm getting a lot of pressure... The Board... The Arts Council... the rest of the Company. |
| PENNY | They don't support me? |
| JACK | They want the problem sorted. |
| PENNY | Well so do I. |
| JACK | Then you'll have to withdraw your membership and publicly denounce that party. |
| PENNY | I can't do it. |

*Pause.*

| | |
|---|---|
| JACK | Penny, we are a publicly funded company... an arts organisation with commitments to race / equality |
| PENNY | I am not racist Jack. |
| JACK | I know that. |
| PENNY | How can you think that? |
| JACK | I don't... Of course I don't. |
| PENNY | My boyfriend's black for God's sake. |

*Pause.*

| | |
|---|---|
| JACK | Your boyfriend? |
| PENNY | |
| JACK | Already? |
| PENNY | It's been three months. |
| JACK | |

29

| | |
|---|---|
| PENNY | I'm sorry, Jack. But life goes on. |
| JACK | Yes, yes of course. |
| PENNY | I thought you'd... moved on. |
| JACK | I have. Of course, I have. |
| PENNY | I'm sorry. |
| JACK | There's nothing to be sorry about. |

*Pause.*

| | |
|---|---|
| PENNY | Jack, you know I'm not racist. |
| JACK | Yes but you're affiliated with an organisation known for its racist ideology. |
| PENNY | Immigration control has nothing to do with racism. |
| JACK | We have many immigrants in the company, Penny. How do you think they feel? |
| PENNY | It's mass immigration I object to. |
| JACK | Look... let's stop there. What matters is the disruptions and how we stop them. |
| PENNY | I can't do it Jack. |
| JACK | You'll be able to dance again. |
| PENNY | I'll look silly. Weak. No backbone. |
| JACK | You were young, naïve, vulnerable. People will see that. |
| PENNY | They'll see someone who hasn't the guts to stand up for what she believes in. |
| JACK | But you don't really believe in it, do you darling? Not deep down? |

*Pause.*

PENNY          I signed up after reading their manifesto...
what do you think?

*Pause.*

JACK           I see.
PENNY          You said it didn't matter.
JACK           It doesn't. Of course, it doesn't.
PENNY          But you'd still like me to withdraw my
membership?
JACK           You haven't much choice.

*Pause.*

PENNY          What happens if I don't?
JACK           Then the problem doesn't go away.
PENNY          Can you stop me from dancing
indefinitely?
JACK           Maybe.
PENNY          Can I be sacked?
JACK           Probably.

*Pause.*

PENNY          Look, just let me dance and they'll
eventually give up.
JACK           They'll have people in the auditorium
ready to stand up and shout abuse every

31

|  | time your foot hits the stage. They guarantee it. |
| PENNY | But they can't possibly keep it up. |
| JACK | Penny, have you seen their Facebook page? They've got hundreds of thousands of supporters and the number grows bigger by the day. |
| PENNY | Bloody Facebook... that's all I hear nowadays. Isn't it just spotty teenagers with too much time on their hands? |
| JACK | These social networking sites are practically bringing down governments, darling. What chance do you think we stand? |

*Pause.*

|  | If we don't do something soon they'll have us closed down by Christmas. |
| PENNY | Come off it, Jack. It can't be that bad. |
| JACK | It is, darling. I promise you. Glenmaddoch have pulled the sponsorship on the Christmas show. Box Office is down fifty eight percent. Our regular funding from the Arts Council is under review. That's how bad it is. |

*Pause.*

| PENNY | Is there no other way? |

| JACK | No. |
| PENNY | Legally, can we do something? |
| JACK | It doesn't seem so. And even if we could, there's no way we can police the people who buy tickets. |

*Pause.*

| PENNY | What would you do? In my position, what would you do? |
| JACK | I wouldn't like it, but I would do what they wanted. |

*Long pause.*

| PENNY | Jack, I feel sick. |
| JACK | I understand. But people will think you've done the right thing. Trust me. |

**FIVE**

*The following week. Penny's press conference. Jack and Penny sitting at a table. The journalists are heard but not seen.*

| PENNY | The recent allegations about me in the press and brought to light by the protests |

33

at our theatre are true. I joined the party when I was young after reading a story about an illegal immigrant who had been driving a car without a licence and had run over and killed a little girl. He was fined sixty five pounds. I was so disgusted and upset that I felt I had to do something. So I read their manifesto and took it on face value. I'm not too proud to say that a lot of it went over my head but some of the things they mentioned were the things I think about all the time, mainly mass immigration, crime and increased taxes. So I signed up. I now know this was naïve of me. Silly. I'm not a political person and I shouldn't have signed up without understanding their full philosophy which contains some very nasty elements. Hence I've now withdrawn my membership and want to apologise, deeply apologise, to the people I've upset. Thank you.

JOURN 1    Are you a racist, Ms Leigh?

JACK    Fellas, please... let's be reasonable here.

PENNY    It's okay Jack. (*Pause*) No I'm not racist.

JOURN 2    Have you now changed your views on the issue of immigration?

PENNY    I still have concerns about immigration... mass immigration. I mean, Britain isn't really very big and I can't see the logic of allowing so many people in and no amount

34

|         |                                                                 |
|---------|-----------------------------------------------------------------|
|         | of personal criticism will make me change my mind about that.   |
| JOURN 1 | Is it true you and your boyfriend have split up over this?       |
| PENNY   | No.                                                             |
| JOURN 2 | What do you say to those people who think you're only doing this to save your career? |
| JACK    | Okay, that's enough questions fellas.                           |
| JOURN 1 | Ms Leigh, is it true you've had to hire a bodyguard?            |
| JOURN 2 | Do you sleep under a union jack duvet, Ms Leigh?               |

*Laughter.*


**SIX**

*Chanting outside. Jack is at his desk reading the newspaper article. The phone rings. He picks it up.*

| JACK | Hi... Yes... I don't know but... If you let me... Trevor! I have arranged a meeting... I'm going to find out... Let's not be hasty... He's on his way... Calm down, Trevor... Let me speak to him first... |

*The door knocks.*

35

Look I think he's here... Yes... straight
after... Right.

*The door knocks again.*

JACK            Come in.

*Mr X enters.*

JACK            Sit down.
MR X            Thank you.
JACK            Mr X let me get straight to the point.
MR X            Of course. Please do.
JACK            Ms Leigh has withdrawn her membership
                and publicly denounced that party, has
                she not?
MR X            Ah... yes. Yes she has, I suppose.
JACK            You saw the press conference?
MR X            Indeed.
JACK            She has done what you requested.
MR X            What my organisation requested.
JACK            Yes, what your organisation requested.
MR X            I am just / the
JACK            Spokesperson, I know.
MR X            We need to be clear on these matters.
JACK            Mr   X,   why   have   the   disruptions
                continued?
MR X            Because our committee felt dissatisfied.
JACK            Dissatisfied?

| | |
|---|---|
| MR X | Oh yes. So we held a meeting. Took a vote. And decided to continue the protests. It was an unanimous decision, Mr Stevens. |
| JACK | Why? |
| MR X | Why? |
| JACK | Why did your organisation feel dissatisfied? |

*Pause.*

| | |
|---|---|
| JACK | Well? |
| MR X | Sorry, I need to find the right word... I'm trying to remember the word which was used. I do this all the time. I'm very forgetful. Please forgive me... Tokenism. Yes, that's it. It was felt that Ms Leigh was insincere. Her apology felt tokenistic. |
| JACK | Ms Leigh very much regrets joining that party. She made that very clear. |
| MR X | She showed no regret. |
| JACK | I'm a personal friend of Ms Leigh's and I assure you she genuinely feels regret about joining that party. |
| MR X | Our committee thinks not. |
| JACK | It's the truth. |

*Pause.*

| | |
|---|---|
| MR X | I have Ms Leigh's statement here... (*He searches in his satchel.*) It reads and I |

quote... oh sorry this is my shopping list. (*He searches again*) Ah, here it is..."I still have great concerns about mass immigration and no amount of personal attack will make me change my mind about that."

JACK          And?

MR X          Her tone is... defiant.

JACK

MR X          Not regretful.

JACK          Alright Mr X, what is it you want?

MR X          My organisation.

JACK          Yes your organisation!

*Pause.*

MR X          The only way forward... the only thing that will satisfy our committee is Ms Leigh's resignation or her dismissal.

JACK

MR X          We have voted.

JACK          Please be reasonable.

MR X          We have voted.

JACK          But surely / there's

MR X          We do not reach these decisions lightly.

JACK          Mr X...

MR X          It was unanimous.

JACK          Please...

MR X          Only Ms Leigh's resignation will satisfy our / members

| | |
|---|---|
| JACK | Mr X, please put yourself in this girl's shoes. She has been made to publicly humiliate herself on TV as well as in the papers. She's hounded by the press on a daily basis. She has been ostracised by the rest of the company and by some of her closest friends. The poor girl is on the brink of a nervous breakdown. Don't you think she's suffered enough? |
| MR X | No one forced Ms Leigh to join that party. |
| JACK | I've known Ms Leigh a long time. Please believe me when I tell you she's practically a child when it comes to politics and intellectual debate. She doesn't deserve this. |

*Pause.*

| | |
|---|---|
| MR X | But we have voted. |
| JACK | Have some compassion. |
| MR X | |
| JACK | Please. |
| MR X | We have voted. |
| JACK | Dancing is the only thing she truly cares about and believes in. |
| MR X | Mr Stevens, we have voted. |
| JACK | Maybe if I spoke to your committee... your members... explain to them... |
| MR X | That will not be possible. |
| JACK | Please. |

| | |
|---|---|
| MR X | |
| JACK | If they hear how this has affected / her… |
| MR X | It won't make a difference. |
| JACK | How about we get Ms Leigh to speak to them directly? |
| MR X | It's too late… we have voted. |
| JACK | There must be some way… |
| MR X | We have voted. |
| JACK | How about we… hold a fund-raising benefit for your organisation… there are loads of ways we could help you out … we could put your logo on our programmes, help advertise your group… |
| MR X | We are not a cancer charity, Mr Stevens. Monetary gain does not interest us and we certainly don't need help in promoting our group. |
| JACK | Please, won't you consider / any other alternative? |
| MR X | We have voted. |
| JACK | Will you please stop saying that! |

*Pause.*

| | |
|---|---|
| JACK | Mr X… |
| MR X | Yes? |
| JACK | Please leave. |

*Pause.*

MR X                    As you wish.

*Mr X stands and goes towards the door.*

MR X                    We    have    voted    to    disrupt    *all*
                        performances,   whether   Ms   Leigh   is   in
                        them or not... until she resigns or is fired
                        from    your    company.    Goodbye,    Mr
                        Stevens.

*He exits. Jack pours himself a whiskey.*




**SEVEN**

*A few days later. Penny paces up and down in the office. Jack
sits at the desk.*

JACK                    Sit down, Penny. Please.
PENNY                   I'm too nervous.
JACK                    Yes, I understand. So am I. But pacing up
                        and down like a caged animal isn't helping
                        matters.
PENNY                   It's helping me.
JACK                    We need to remain calm.
PENNY                   Easy for you to say.
JACK                    Please just sit down and try to relax a
                        little. I'll get you a drink.

| | |
|---|---|
| PENNY | Make it a double. |
| JACK | Of course. |

*He makes her and himself a drink.*

| | |
|---|---|
| PENNY | It's not going to work, Jack. |
| JACK | If anyone can get him to change his mind, you can. |
| PENNY | He'll walk out as soon as he sees me. |
| JACK | I won't let him. |
| PENNY | What will you do? Wrestle him to the ground and tie his hands behind his back? |
| JACK | If I have to. |
| PENNY | Serious Jack. If he turns and walks out, what do we do? |
| JACK | He won't. |
| PENNY | He might. |
| JACK | Then you'll have to use your powers of persuasion to get him to stay. |
| PENNY | He's ruined my life. How can I possibly sit here and be nice to him? |
| JACK | No-ones asking you to be nice. Just be honest. Tell him how the whole thing's affected you. Tell him how you never really understood their manifesto. Make him see you've suffered enough. |
| PENNY | Be a victim, you mean. |
| JACK | Well, yes. |
| PENNY | I'm not sure I can go through with it. |
| JACK | You'll have to. |

| | |
|---|---|
| PENNY | Do I really? |
| JACK | Pretend it's a performance. |
| PENNY | That doesn't help, Jack. |
| JACK | I've seen how you cast a spell over the critics on press nights. Just do the same here. |
| PENNY | It's not the same. |
| JACK | It's seduction whatever way you look at it, darling. And I for one can remember how seductive and charming you can be. |

*The door knocks.*

| | |
|---|---|
| PENNY | Shit! |
| JACK | Remain calm. |

*Jack answers the door.*

Mr X, please come in.

*Mr X enters. When he sees Penny he stops.*

| | |
|---|---|
| MR X | We have not... not agreed to this, Mr Stevens. |
| JACK | I know but Penny wanted to speak to you in person. |
| PENNY | Mr / X |
| MR X | You have tricked me. You have made me come here under false pretences. I cannot allow this meeting to take place. |

43

| | |
|---|---|
| PENNY | Mr X, please. Hear me out. Just a couple of minutes. Please. |
| MR X | My organisation has not agreed to this meeting, Ms Leigh, therefore I cannot stay. I'm very sorry. |
| PENNY | Just a minute, please. |
| JACK | You're here now. You might as well stay to hear what she's got to say. |
| MR X | Decisions have been made. Nothing you can say will affect that. |
| PENNY | Does your organisation know what I've gone through in the past few weeks, Mr X? Do they know how many great friends I've lost? How I've had to change my telephone number three times? How my sick mother can't leave her front door without being trampled on by the press?

Do you know what it's like having to live with the blinds closed? Afraid to go into the hallway to pick up the mail in case there's another package filled with human excrement? Or afraid to open the newspaper in case there's another spiteful lie being told about you?

I have suffered enough Mr X. If I'm forced to resign it will completely destroy me. Is that fair? That I lose everything because of a stupid mistake I made when I was |

young, and which I now totally regret. And please believe me, I'm not just saying I regret it because of what's happening to me now. I'm saying it because I genuinely despise many of that organisation's philosophies which I didn't really comprehend at the time.

*Pause.*

| | |
|---|---|
| MR X | Many? |
| PENNY | Sorry? |
| MR X | You said *many of* that organisation's philosophies. Meaning not all. |
| PENNY | |
| MR X | Do you mean there's some of their philosophies you agree with? |
| PENNY | |
| MR X | Ms Leigh? |
| PENNY | |
| JACK | Of course she doesn't. |
| MR X | What about immigration? |
| PENNY | |
| MR X | Do you still support their views on immigration, Ms Leigh? |
| PENNY | |
| JACK | Of course, she doesn't. Tell him, Penny. |
| PENNY | |
| JACK | Tell him. |
| PENNY | |

| | |
|---|---|
| JACK | For God's sake, Penny. |
| MR X | Thank you, Ms Leigh. I'll report back to my committee. Truthfully, I can't see that anything will change. |
| JACK | Mr X... |

*Mr X exits.*

| | |
|---|---|
| PENNY | |
| JACK | You could have lied. |
| PENNY | I couldn't. |
| JACK | You should have lied. |
| PENNY | No. |
| JACK | This is you all over. You say you want one thing but your actions prove the opposite. |
| PENNY | And what's that supposed to mean? |
| JACK | Nothing. I'm sorry. |
| PENNY | I want them to stop the protests, yes. But not at any cost. |
| JACK | One little lie, Penny. That's all it would have taken. |
| PENNY | He would have seen right through it. |
| JACK | It was worth a try. |
| PENNY | No it wasn't. |

*Pause.*

| | |
|---|---|
| JACK | You'll have to resign. You know that, don't you? |
| PENNY | No. |

46

| | |
|---|---|
| JACK | They've got us by the short and curlies. |
| PENNY | I will not resign, Jack. |

*Pause.*

| | |
|---|---|
| JACK | We can fire you. |
| PENNY | |
| JACK | We've taken advice, legal advice. And we can fire you if we have to. |
| PENNY | Well thanks. Thanks a lot. |
| JACK | We don't want to do it, but we can if we have to. |
| PENNY | Under what grounds? |
| JACK | Your continued employment is jeopardising the future of the company. It threatens to bankrupt us and make a lot of people unemployed. |
| PENNY | It's not me. It's them. |
| JACK | I'm just giving you the legal picture, Penny. The grounds for your dismissal if we have to use it. |
| PENNY | I'll get a lawyer. The top lawyer. The best. You can't screw me around like this. |
| JACK | I understand your anger. We share it. But... we haven't got much choice. |
| PENNY | I can't believe this. I can't believe what's happening. |
| JACK | I know. |
| PENNY | I've given everything to this Company. Danced in every flea-ridden shit-hole you |

47

|  |  |
|---|---|
|  | sent me to without a word of complaint. Attended every press conference. Wine and dined every bloody fat funder when I was asked to. I've never had a day off sick even though every month I go through hell wanting nothing more than to lie in bed with a hot water bottle pressed against my guts... |
| JACK | I know... |
| PENNY | And all the sacrifices I've made... no holidays... no drinking... no eating for Christ's sake and all because I wanted to be the best, cos I wanted the company to be the best, cos I wanted you to be proud of me. And the baby... |
| JACK | Penny let's / not |
| PENNY | We sacrificed our baby / for this |
| JACK | Penny don't. |
| PENNY | We need to talk about it, Jack. |
| JACK | No. Let's just concentrate on what's going on now. (*Pause*) Look, give me a couple of days to see if I can come up with something. I'll talk to Trevor, the Board, our legal team. See if there's any other way out of this. So try not to worry. I'm sure there's something we can do. |

*Pause.*

| PENNY | They shouldn't be allowed to do this. |

48

| JACK | I know. |
| PENNY | We have to stand up to them. |
| JACK | Yes. Yes, darling we do. |

## EIGHT

*Trevor and Jack sit staring at each other. Finally...*

| TREVOR | We had a Board meeting last night. |
| JACK | Oh. (*Pause*) Why wasn't I asked to attend? |
| TREVOR | Why do you think? |
| JACK | I should have been asked. |

*Pause.*

| TREVOR | We're going to fire her. |
| JACK | I thought I was responsible for all the hiring and firing around here. |
| TREVOR | In this case, it was felt you were... incapable of making an objective decision. |
| JACK | And you agreed with that? |
| TREVOR | She's your ex, Jack. You're very close. You were in love. You were going to start a family. It's understandable. |
| JACK | What's understandable? |
| TERVOR | Oh come on. |
| JACK | No, tell me. |

49

| | |
|---|---|
| TREVOR | I'm not playing these games. |
| JACK | My loyalty is to the company. I want what's best for the Company. And giving into these people is not what's best for this Company. |
| TREVOR | We're on the brink of bankruptcy. You can't let your feelings for Penny get in the way. She has to go. |
| JACK | My feelings for Penny have nothing to do with it. I just don't like what these people are doing. It's not right. We live in a democracy for goodness sake, not some bloody Orwellian state. We can't let them win, Trevor, don't you see that. |
| TREVOR | But they have. |
| JACK | Don't be so defeatist. We haven't even tried to fight back. |
| TREVOR | Oh come on Jack. You heard what Martin said. There's nothing we can do. If we go through the courts it will take forever, meanwhile we keep bleeding bucketfuls of money. |
| JACK | And what if Penny sues us for unfair dismissal? |
| TREVOR | It's easier to fight an individual than a whole bloody army. |

*Pause.*

50

| | |
|---|---|
| JACK | Give me two more days, Trevor. Before doing anything. Please. |
| TREVOR | What for? It's useless. |
| JACK | Just a couple of days, Trevor. I deserve that much. Penny deserves that much. |
| TREVOR | The Board was adamant. They won't change their minds. |
| JACK | Then don't tell them. |
| TREVOR | |
| JACK | You owe me, Trevor. I don't want to say it, but if it wasn't for me you wouldn't be around today. That must count for something |

*Pause.*

| | |
|---|---|
| TREVOR | Okay, Jack. But I have to warn you... Some members of the Board – and you probably know who - are calling for your blood as well. They never liked the fact you and Penny were together in the first place and now this... If you don't come up with something in two days, I can't guarantee you'll have a job, never mind Penny. |

*He gets up to leave.*

| | |
|---|---|
| JACK | Thanks, Trevor. |

TREVOR      If I have another bloody coronary, I'm
            blaming you.

*Trevor exits. Jack pours himself a drink. He paces up and
down the office stopping every so often to look at the posters.
Suddenly he has an idea. He picks up the phone.*

JACK        Taz dear, what time is it in Australia?


**NINE**

*Two days later. Penny sits in the office, cleaning something
off her jacket with a paper towel. She's upset. Jack enters.*

JACK        Sorry I'm late, darling. The traffic was a
            bloody nightmare.

*He sits down opposite her.*

            What's happened? Are you alright?

PENNY       Someone threw a yoghurt at me. In
            Waitrose. They threw a peach flavoured
            yoghurt and shouted Nazi bitch.

*She starts to cry.*

JACK        I'm so sorry, Penny.

*He goes to comfort her.*

PENNY        Don't touch me. I couldn't bear it.

JACK        Do you want a drink?

PENNY        I want it to end, Jack.

JACK        Yes, so do we. And I think I've come up with a solution.

PENNY        What is it?

JACK        You will resign from the company...

PENNY        No.

JACK        Just hear me out.

PENNY        No, Jack. I will not resign.

JACK        Penny, please. Just listen to what I've got to say.

PENNY        I'm not going to resign.

JACK        You will resign from the company and in a month's time, when everything has died down, you'll be appointed principal dancer of our sister company in Sydney. I've arranged it.

PENNY        Sydney?

JACK        Yes.

PENNY        Australia?

JACK        It's a fantastic opportunity.

PENNY        Don't be ridiculous, Jack.

JACK        Just think about it.

PENNY        I can't go to Australia. What about mum? It could be cancer. Her bones. I have to be here. My life is here, Jack.

| | |
|---|---|
| JACK | With the salary you'll be on, you could come back every month. Or Marion could go with you. The sun will be good for her. And the medical care out there is so much better than here. |
| PENNY | My dog. I couldn't leave little Luna. And what about Trent? He's just moved in. I think it might work. We get on so well together. |

*Pause.*

| | |
|---|---|
| JACK | Take time... think about it. |
| PENNY | I don't need to think about it. I'm not going. |
| JACK | It's your only option. |
| PENNY | Australia is the other side of the world. |
| JACK | It's only twenty-four hours away. |
| PENNY | I hate Australian's! The men, the accents... all that bloody blonde hair and white teeth. The sun... even the bloody sun I hate. |
| JACK | The Company, Penny. Think about the Company. Their reputation grows year by year. |
| PENNY | They're second-rate. |
| JACK | They're cutting edge. |
| PENNY | They're crap and you know it. |
| JACK | Penny, I'm trying my best here to save your bloody career. |

54

| | |
|---|---|
| PENNY | Suggesting I fly to the back end of nowhere to dance with a bunch of rednecks is not saving my career. |
| JACK | Sydney is hardly the back end of nowhere. It's one of the most exciting cities on the planet. Some people would kill for an opportunity like this. |
| PENNY | I'm not going. Nor am I resigning. |

*Pause.*

| | |
|---|---|
| JACK | Please... just think about it. |
| PENNY | No. |

*Pause.*

| | |
|---|---|
| JACK | If you don't go for this, Penny, you'll be fired. |
| PENNY | |
| JACK | And no other company will hire you, knowing the trouble it may cause. So please... reconsider. |

*Pause.*

| | |
|---|---|
| PENNY | You're asking me to give up too much, Jack. |
| JACK | But you'll be able to dance. Isn't that what's important? |

*Pause.*

PENNY        I don't want to go.

*Pause.*

JACK         Penny darling, I'm going to speak
             honestly now. You're not getting any
             younger. At most you have another five
             years left before retirement. Do you really
             want to throw those years away?

*Pause.*

PENNY        But I don't want to go, Jack.
JACK
PENNY        Please, don't make me.
JACK         It's our only option.
PENNY        No, Jack. I'm not going. I don't want to
             go.
JACK         But you want to dance, don't you?

*Long pause.*

JACK         They're so excited about you going over.
             And Giselle's their next production. How
             great is that?

**TEN**

*Six weeks later. Jack is pacing up and down and on the phone.*

JACK          Yes, it was my idea to send her... but you agreed. You all agreed. You said you thought it was a great solution. You congratulated... I will not lose my job over this. I will not be made a scapegoat... Yes, it is a fucking threat!

*He slams the phone down and has a drink of whiskey. The door knocks.*

JACK          Come in.

*Mr X enters. He remains standing. Jack doesn't speak.*

MR X         Shall I sit down?
JACK
MR X         Oh dear, I can see you're upset. Maybe I should come back another time.
JACK         So. Disruptions are now taking place in Sydney.
MR X         Yes.
JACK         As well as continuing here.
MR X         Well, yes. What did you expect?

*He sits down.*

57

| | |
|---|---|
| JACK | Even though you got what you wanted. |
| MR X | *We* did not get what *we* wanted. |
| JACK | Ms Leigh is no longer employed by us. |
| MR X | Yes but Ms Leigh is still employed. |
| JACK | Not by us. |
| MR X | By your sister company. |
| JACK | Artistically we have connections but I can assure you we are very separate organisations. |
| MR X | Our committee disagrees. |
| JACK | We have a different board and a different constitution. |
| MR X | You are still known as sister companies within the dance world. |
| JACK | Legally, financially, in every way we are separate companies. |
| MR X | We disagree. |
| JACK | If the Australian Company wants to employ Ms Leigh that is their decision. |
| MR X | We disagree. |
| JACK | It has nothing to do with us. |
| MR X | We believe you helped secure Ms Leigh's employment with your Australian company. |
| JACK | It is not *our* Australian company. |
| MR X | Alright, we believe you helped secure Ms Leigh's employment with *the* Australian company. |
| JACK | We supplied references yes. Legally and morally we were obliged to. There was |

|         |                                                                                 |
|---------|---------------------------------------------------------------------------------|
|         | nothing wrong with Ms Leigh's dancing abilities.                                |
| MR X    | We find it unacceptable that Ms Leigh is still employed as a dancer for a high profile company given her political views. |
| JACK    | That is not our problem anymore.                                                |
| MR X    | That is not for you to decide.                                                  |
| JACK    | What do you mean?                                                               |
| MR X    | Our members will decide if it's your problem.                                   |
| JACK    | This is intolerable.                                                            |
| MR X    | And we have voted.                                                              |
| JACK    |                                                                                 |
| MR X    | We have voted to continue our protests until Ms Leigh is no longer employed as a dancer at your sister company in Sydney… |
| JACK    | This is ridiculous.                                                             |
| MR X    | Or any other company.                                                           |
| JACK    | Don't be absurd man.                                                            |
| MR X    | It is within your company's power to keep Ms Leigh from gaining further employment as a dancer. Our protests will continue until this has happened. |

*Pause.*

| JACK | Why are you intent on destroying this company and this girl's life? |
|------|---------------------------------------------------------------------|

59

| | |
|---|---|
| MR X | Oh that is not our intention, Mr Stevens. Not at all. Our intention is to wipe-out right-wing ideology wherever we find it. |
| JACK | It's nothing more than a witch-hunt. |
| MR X | Right wing ideology leads to fascism. It leads to young innocent teenagers being blown away by a madman on an island in Norway. It must be stamped out wherever and whenever it raises its ugly head. |
| JACK | We are taking about one naïve girl here. |
| MR X | Some thought Hitler was naïve until he invaded Poland. |
| JACK | This is preposterous. |
| MR X | Our members think not. |
| JACK | Fuck your members! |

*Pause.*

| | |
|---|---|
| MR X | Let me reiterate… it is within your company's power to stop Ms Leigh from dancing in Sydney and from gaining further employment as a dancer anywhere else. Our protests will continue until this has occurred. |
| JACK | I will not let you blackmail us like this. The law of the land will not allow this to happen. |
| MR X | The law, I'm afraid, is powerless when it comes to this type of direct action. |
| JACK | We'll see. |

*Pause.*

MR X            Mr Stevens, did you know our members
                number over two million world-wide? Over
                a   million   in   this   country   alone.
                Extraordinary, isn't it? (*Pause*) Do you
                really think the law can stop us?
JACK            By God I'm going to make sure they try.
MR X            You will fail. And even if you don't, it will
                take a very long time. Meanwhile, your
                company will continue to lose / money
JACK            Get out.
MR X            It will be forced to / close…
JACK            Get out now.
MR X            As well as your sister company in Sydney.
JACK            Get out you disgusting little man!

*Mr X jumps up thinking Jack is going to hit him. He moves
towards the door but then realises he's left his satchel at the side
of the chair.*

MR X            My satchel.

*Jack fetches the satchel and throws it at him.*

JACK            Get out.

*As Mr X is about to leave he stops.*

| | |
|---|---|
| MR X | Mr Stevens, we must strive to maintain a modicum of professionalism at all times. Goodbye. |

*He exits. Jack throws the whiskey glass and smashes it against the picture of Giselle.*


**ELEVEN**

*A week later. Penny and Jack are in the office standing opposite each other. Penny slaps him hard across the face.*

| | |
|---|---|
| PENNY | Coward! Fucking coward! |
| JACK | I'm sorry… |
| PENNY | What do I do now? Tell me. Tell me that. |
| JACK | I don't know. It's out of my control. |
| PENNY | No one will touch me. |
| JACK | I know. |
| PENNY | All the people I thought I could rely on… all the people who begged me, offered me the world to leave this company and work for them… won't even answer my phone calls… |
| JACK | I'm sorry. |
| PENNY | I couldn't even get a job on a cruise liner now if I wanted to. Is that fair, Jack? |
| JACK | No. No it's not. |
| PENNY | You have to do something. |
| JACK | There's nothing I can / do |

| | |
|---|---|
| PENNY | You have to do something! I went to Australia for you. I spent two months in that sun-drenched hell-hole while my mother lay dying... and for what? To be turfed out on my ear. |
| JACK | They had no choice. |
| PENNY | I'm sick of hearing that Jack. I'm sick of it. |
| JACK | I don't know what to say. |
| PENNY | I don't want you to say anything, I want you to do something. You owe me. |
| JACK | Do you need money? |
| PENNY | I don't need money, I need a fucking job. I need to dance. |
| JACK | I can't help you Penny. No dance company will go near you. They can't take the risk |
| PENNY | You could re-employ me. |
| JACK | I can't. Even if I wanted to the Board wouldn't allow it. |
| PENNY | After all I've done for this company. |
| JACK | Yes. I'm sorry. (*Pause*) Have you thought about teaching? |
| PENNY | Teaching? |
| JACK | Yes. There's nothing wrong in that. You could open up your own school. Pass on your skills. I could help you finance it. No-one need know about it. |
| PENNY | Fuck you! |
| JACK | I'm trying to help Penny. |

63

| | |
|---|---|
| PENNY | I'm sure you are. |
| JACK | I've been fighting tooth and nail for you. |
| PENNY | I find that hard to believe. |
| JACK | How can you say that? |
| PENNY | I wouldn't be surprised if it was you who leaked the story to that man and his bloody organisation in the first place. |
| JACK | I knew nothing about your membership to that party. |
| PENNY | I bet you've been trying to get rid of me ever since we split up. |
| JACK | Be reasonable Penny. You're talking nonsense now. |
| PENNY | You're jealous I've been getting on with my life, that I've met someone else. |
| JACK | You're being ridiculous. |
| PENNY | Is this payback for what happened, Jack? |
| JACK | Just stop. |
| PENNY | Because every time I walk down the street and see a new mother with her baby I get my punishment tenfold. |
| JACK | Shut up, Penny. |
| PENNY | I will not be blamed for what happened Jack. Not any more. |
| JACK | No-one blames you. |
| PENNY | I know you do. I can see it in your eyes. |
| JACK | I'm not being drawn into this again. |
| PENNY | We need to talk about it. |
| JACK | No! There's no point dragging ourselves through the mill again. Now please... just |

leave, Penny. There's nothing more I can do for you.

*Pause.*

PENNY          I will not be a victim anymore. Someone is going to pay for what's happened to me.

*She exits.*

**TWELVE**

*Jack is drinking whiskey. Trevor enters.*

TREVOR          So the bitch has gone ahead and done it.
JACK            Trevor... what are you talking about?

*He throws a letter onto Jack's desk.*

TREVOR          As if you don't know.

*Jack takes the letter and reads.*

                Did you encourage her to do this?
JACK            For God's sake, why would I? Don't you think I've gone through enough?
TREVOR          That Judas Nazi bitch turning on the family that made her.

| | |
|---|---|
| JACK | I warned you something like this would happen. It was to be expected. |
| TREVOR | I thought you'd be able to prevent it. You said you knew how to play her. You said you were still close. |
| JACK | That was before all this happened. |
| TREVOR | Can't you do something? |
| JACK | She's angry. I can't say I blame her. |
| TREVOR | So you're on her side? |
| JACK | I didn't say that. |
| TREVOR | Well that's what it sounds like. |
| JACK | Calm down Trevor, this is helping no-one. Here have a drink. |

*He pours him a drink.*

| | |
|---|---|
| TREVOR | I'm sick of it Jack. Sick of the whole rotten business. Why should I be piggy-in-the-middle between you and the Board all the time? It isn't fair? They've used the fact that we're personal friends to get me to do their dirty work for them. Well, I've had enough. I'm going to resign. |
| JACK | Come on now. Stop feeling sorry for yourself. You love this company. Think of all those gorgeous young men in tights you get to spend time with. Where else could that happen? |

*He smiles.*

| | |
|---|---|
| TREVOR | Can't you speak to her, dear boy? |
| JACK | It won't make a difference. |
| TREVOR | Ask her to marry you or something. Tell her you want to try for a family again. Tell her anything, for Christ's sake. |
| JACK | She's got someone else. |
| TREVOR | Oh. Serious? |
| JACK | I think so. |
| TREVOR | Then we're up shit street. |
| JACK | What have the Board said? |
| TREVOR | We're going to fight her. We've got no other bloody choice. |
| JACK | And what about me? |

*Pause.*

| | |
|---|---|
| TREVOR | When your contract is up in July, you won't be asked to re-apply. |
| JACK | |
| TREVOR | I did what I could, dear boy... but... they're convinced you knew about Penny's political persuasion right from the beginning. They blame you for getting us into this mess. |

*Pause.*

| | |
|---|---|
| JACK | I suppose there's no point in trying to change their minds? |
| TREVOR | None whatsoever. |

*The phone rings.*

JACK          Yes... What does he want..? Tell him I'm
              busy... Tell him again, Taz. Oh for God's
              sake...

*He puts the phone down.*

TREVOR        What is it?
JACK          Our friend Mr X.
TREVOR        What the fuck does he want?
JACK          We're about to find out.

*There's a knock. Jack gets up and opens the door.*

              Well if it isn't the enigmatic Mr X.

*He indicates for him to enter, which he does.*

MR X          Oh... you're busy...
TREVOR        Don't mind me. I'm just one of the
              Director's of the Company you've fucking
              destroyed.
MR X          Can we speak alone?
TREVOR        Anything you've got to say to Jack you
              can say to me.
JACK          Your demands have been met. I don't
              think there's anything else to say. Do you?
MR X          We need to speak. It's in your best
              interests that we speak.

| | |
|---|---|
| TREVOR | Why don't you just sod off back to the little hole in the ground you crawled out off, you fucking weasel. |
| JACK | Trevor / |
| TREVOR | People like you make me sick... you're so fucking smug... you think you're morally superior to everyone else. You walk around looking down your noses at people or pitying us from your ivory fucking towers. Then you go home, close the door and kick the living daylights out of your wives, or masturbate to children getting raped on / the internet |
| JACK | Trevor that's / enough |
| TREVOR | I know your sort Mr X and your hypocrisy makes me sick. |

*Mr X stares at Trevor but then speaks calmly to Jack.*

| | |
|---|---|
| MR X | This is important, Mr Stevens. |
| TREVOR | We don't want to hear it. There's nothing more you can do to us, so piss off. |
| JACK | Trevor, maybe you should leave. |
| TREVOR | What? |
| JACK | Let me hear what he has to say. |
| TREVOR | Are you mad? |
| JACK | I'll give you a call afterwards. |
| TREVOR | Why should we give / him |
| JACK | Trevor... go on. I'll handle it. |

*Pause.*

TREVOR            Okay, Jack. But don't let him bully you
                  anymore.

*Trevor exits.*

JACK              So... what is it?
MR X              We have held a ballot.
JACK              I don't care if you've held a line dancing
                  competition.
MR X              Our committee has voted to resume the
                  protests.
JACK
MR X              The protests are to resume tomorrow
                  night.
JACK
MR X              Your company is on the brink of
                  bankruptcy. Your management of the
                  situation has been publicly criticised and
                  your own position within the company
                  probably hangs on a thread. Surely you
                  must be interested in eradicating the
                  problem for good.

*Pause.*

JACK              Get out.
MR X              I don't think you mean that.

| | |
|---|---|
| JACK | The problem has been solved. Now get out. |
| MR X | No... no... the problem has not been solved... not completely. |
| JACK | Ms Leigh's dancing career is over. |
| MR X | Yes that is true, I agree. But our committee feels... insecure. |
| JACK | Oh do they indeed? |
| MR X | They still feel Ms Leigh has plenty of opportunities to promote her dangerous beliefs. She could start teaching. She could open up for own school. Future generations of dancers are in danger of having their minds tainted by this woman's pernicious views. Hence we want the problem... eradicated. |
| JACK | Eradicated? |
| MR X | Yes. We want the problem to disappear... for good. As I'm sure you do. |
| JACK | I don't quite understand... |
| MR X | We want to problem to go away permanently. |
| JACK | What do you mean? |
| MR X | We mean... we want the problem to go away permanently. |

*Jack starts to laugh.*

| | |
|---|---|
| JACK | Oh please... get out. |

| | |
|---|---|
| MR X | The protests will resume tomorrow night until the problem has been eradicated. |
| JACK | Get out of my sight! |

*Mr X exits.*


**THIRTEEN**

*The following night. Jack drinks whiskey. Penny stands looking at him. The letter from the previous scene is on the desk in front of him.*

| | |
|---|---|
| JACK | Thanks for coming at such short notice. |
| PENNY | It's late. |
| JACK | I know. I'm sorry. I just... needed to see you. |
| PENNY | How many of those have you had? |
| JACK | Only a couple. |

*Pause.*

Alright, a few.

*He laughs.*

| | |
|---|---|
| PENNY | What? |
| JACK | You always hated it when I drank. |

72

*Pause.*

|         | Remember the night in that grotty little bar near Mariinsky's... what was it called? Molotov, that's it. |
|---------|----------------------------------------------------------------------------------------------------------|
| PENNY   | It was Moloko. |
| JACK    | Yes, you're right. And I got the whole place to sing Happy Birthday to you when it wasn't even your birthday. And you wanted the earth to swallow you up. Remember? |
| PENNY   | |
| JACK    | And then in the hotel afterwards... we had that massive argument that ended in the best sex ever. |
| PENNY   | Jack, stop it. |
| JACK    | What? |
| PENNY   | I know what you're trying to do and it's not going to work. |
| JACK    | Look, I just want us to talk like we used to. |
| PENNY   | I'm not going to change my mind... about anything. |
| JACK    | Of course not. I just want to talk. |
| PENNY   | I'm not sure I'm allowed. |
| JACK    | What do you mean? |
| PENNY   | My solicitor has advised me not to. |
| JACK    | Ah, the great Claudius Fisher himself. I must admit I'm impressed. |

| | |
|---|---|
| PENNY | He's a lovely man. They call him Jaws, you know. |
| JACK | It must be costing you an arm and a leg. |
| PENNY | It's worth it. |
| JACK | Is it? Is it really? |
| PENNY | Yes. |

*Pause.*

| | |
|---|---|
| JACK | Look... Penny, is all this necessary? Do you really want to do this? |

*He picks up the letter and reads.*

| | |
|---|---|
| | I mean, constructive dismissal? Bullying and harassment? Intimidation? (*Pause*) Is that fair? |
| PENNY | My career has been destroyed. |
| JACK | Not by us. |
| PENNY | You had a duty to protect me. As an employer. |
| JACK | I tried. We tried. You know that. |
| PENNY | My life has been destroyed through no fault of my own. I can't just lie down and take it. |
| JACK | I understand that / but |
| PENNY | Someone has to pay. |
| JACK | But us, Penny. We're your family. |
| PENNY | I've been treated badly. |

74

| | |
|---|---|
| JACK | I know that but are we really the ones to blame? The company that made you, that nurtured you. (*Pause*) It wasn't us, now was it? It was them. |
| PENNY | But they weren't my employers, Jack. |
| JACK | Okay even if the Company was partly to blame, what about me? I did everything for you and now I'm going to lose my job over this. (*Pause*) Don't you care what happens to me? |
| PENNY | I'm sorry Jack, but I've got no other choice. |
| JACK | You, more than anyone, know how hard I've worked for this position. Does our past count for nothing? |
| PENNY | |
| JACK | Penny, I still care for you. I'll always care for you. Even after all this, you're still my little Giselle. You know that, right? |
| PENNY | Don't… |
| JACK | And I know you still care for me. I can see it in your eyes. |
| PENNY | That's not true. |
| JACK | Oh come on, Penny. Can you honestly say you've got no feelings for me anymore? Be truthful now. |
| PENNY | I don't Jack. |

*Pause.*

| PENNY | I'm sorry. (*Pause*) I better go. |
|---|---|
| JACK | Penny wait. Look, I know you. I know that in normal circumstances you wouldn't dream of doing this to the Company... to me. But... you're feeling hurt and angry... raw. Marion has just recently died... |
| PENNY | Don't you dare. |
| JACK | I'm sorry but it's relevant. |
| PENNY | My mother has nothing to do with this. |
| JACK | Penny what I'm saying / is |
| PENNY | I know what you're saying. |
| JACK | You need to give yourself time, time to recover. You shouldn't be making such decisions in this state... decisions that you may regret in the future. |
| PENNY | Don't patronise me Jack. |
| JACK | I'm not. |
| PENNY | You always speak to me like I'm a child. |
| JACK | Sorry / I don't mean to. |
| PENNY | Even when we were together you were more like my father than a partner. |
| JACK | Alright Penny. |
| PENNY | Your little Giselle... I hate it when you call me that... like I'm your little pet Chihuahua or something. |
| JACK | That's enough. |
| PENNY | Oh I used to play along with it just to make you happy, just to make you feel all |

|         |                                                                 |
|---------|-----------------------------------------------------------------|
|         | powerful and needed. But guess what Jack? I'm no longer your little Giselle. |
| JACK    | I know that.                                                    |
| PENNY   | Then start treating me like a bloody adult.                    |
| JACK    | I'll start treating you like an adult when you stop acting like a child! You know this case against us is a silly attempt at getting some kind of revenge. Well, it's not going to work. It will bankrupt you and it will bankrupt us. There'll be no winners in this game except the bloody lawyers and those lot who started all this trouble in the first place. So please stop thinking about your own ego for once and think about the consequences of your actions. |
| PENNY   | Fuck you, Jack.                                                |
| JACK    | For God's sake Penny, I don't think you realise the stress I'm / under here |
| PENNY   | The stress you're / under...                                   |
| JACK    | I've been getting it from every side. Trevor never stops calling, telling me to sort it out, threatening me... Then there's the Arts Council, the press, those other bastards and now you. Haven't you ever stopped to think about how all this has been affecting me? |
| PENNY   | No Jack! Because I've been too busy trying to hold onto my sanity, too busy trying to find a job. And too busy trying to fend off every right thinking citizen who |

77

thinks it's okay to attack me in the street for having beliefs that differ from their own.

JACK        We are not responsible for that. We were between a rock and a hard place.

PENNY       Boo hoo! I'm the one who's lost everything here. I'm the one who's been tossed out on my ear by my so called family after devoting years of my life / to them...

JACK        Oh stop going on about what you've done for this company! It makes me nauseous! It was all for yourself, for your reputation, your career. Have the balls to admit it, for fuck sake. You never cared about this company or me – you used both of us to get to the top, so stop pretending otherwise.

PENNY       How can you say that after the sacrifices I've made?

JACK        Sacrifices? You willingly got rid of anything that stood in the way of your glowing career... including our child!

PENNY

JACK        It's true.

PENNY       I got rid of that baby because of you! Because you wanted me to. Because you wanted me to do that stupid new Ballet of yours. We need a name, you said. Only my little Giselle can do it justice, you said.

78

| | |
|---|---|
| JACK | I was perfectly happy to go with Christina. But your bloody pride and ambition wouldn't let her do it. |
| PENNY | Liar! |
| JACK | You practically ran to that abortion clinic and got rid of our baby, Penny. And you didn't even have the decency to discuss it with me. |
| PENNY | Because I didn't want you to have the guilt! |
| JACK | No. Because you didn't want me to change your mind! |
| PENNY | That's not true. |
| JACK | Stop deluding yourself. |
| PENNY | I wanted that baby so much. |
| JACK | So did I. |
| PENNY | Then why didn't you say? |
| JACK | Coz I could see you didn't. |
| PENNY | I've always wanted a family. |
| JACK | Don't make me laugh. |

*She slaps him.*

| | |
|---|---|
| JACK | I'm glad I didn't have a child with a stupid selfish racist bitch like you! |
| PENNY | And I'm glad I didn't have it with a yellow-bellied, wishy-washy liberal bastard like you! |

79

JACK          You're a spoilt little fascist and you
              deserve everything that's happened to
              you!
PENNY         Yeah, well watch this spoilt little fascist
              take you and this company to the cleaners!

*She goes to leave.*

JACK          Oh no you don't.

*Jack runs to her and grabs her by the throat.*

PENNY         Jack? Jack... Jack...

*He strangles her. She falls to the floor. He sits down, shocked.
Gradually he recovers and has a couple of glasses of whiskey.
He then trails her body out of the office.*


**FOURTEEN**

*Two months later. A picture of Sleeping Beauty is on the wall.
Trevor opens a bottle of champagne and fills two glasses. He
raises a glass to the picture of Sleeping Beauty and takes a
drink. Jack enters.*

JACK          Trevor... what's going on?

*Trevor raises a glass.*

| | |
|---|---|
| TREVOR | Thirty percent! |
| JACK | What? |
| TREVOR | We're up thirty percent, dear boy. |
| JACK | Really? |
| TREVOR | Really. So come and celebrate. |

*Trevor gives him a glass of champagne.*

| | |
|---|---|
| JACK | I can't believe it. |
| TREVOR | It's all been down to you! |
| JACK | Thanks Trevor, but I think Anastasia might have something to do with it. |
| TREVOR | Yes our little Russian doll is certainly bringing them in. |
| JACK | We were lucky to get her. |
| TREVOR | All down to you – you smooth talking bastard. |
| JACK | One does what one can. |
| TREVOR | She's a looker, isn't she? |
| JACK | You could say that. |
| TREVOR | I hope you're not giving her one, dear boy. |
| JACK | Of course not. |
| TREVOR | Are you sure? |
| JACK | Yes. (*Pause*) Why? |
| TREVOR | Oh nothing. Just that someone spotted you in Brannigan's after the show the other night. |
| JACK | It was only a meal. |
| TREVOR | |
| JACK | One meal, Trevor. |

| | |
|---|---|
| TREVOR | Good. I know you're not the type to make the same mistake twice. |

*Pause.*

| | |
|---|---|
| | Any news of Penny yet? |
| JACK | No. |
| TREVOR | It can't be good. |
| JACK | No. |
| TREVOR | Poor Penny. |
| JACK | Yes. It's terrible. |
| TREVOR | And how are you holding up? |
| JACK | Oh, okay. I've got Luna to keep me busy. |
| TREVOR | Luna? |
| JACK | Her dog. |
| TREVOR | That's good of you. |
| JACK | Didn't want the little thing to go into a home or be put down. It was the least I could do. And anyway, what if Penny does turn up? She loves that dog. |
| TREVOR | You were a good friend to that girl. |
| JACK | She's my little Giselle. |
| TREVOR | To Penny... wherever she may be. |

*He raises his glass and so does Jack.*

| | |
|---|---|
| JACK | To Penny. |

*Pause.*

| | |
|---|---|
| TREVOR | I've been meaning to ask you, dear boy, what did that weasel Mr X want the last time he came in here? |
| JACK | Oh... I can't really remember now... to be honest. Whatever it was, it mustn't have been important. |

*Pause.*

| | |
|---|---|
| TREVOR | It seemed important. |
| JACK | Everything with him seemed important. |
| TREVOR | I thought he was going to make another demand. |
| JACK | Oh God, no. He'd got what he wanted. Hadn't he? |
| TREVOR | Yes... Anyhow, let's not think about him today. I've got some other good news for you. The Board have recommended and agreed to a pay rise. For all your hard work in netting us the wonderful Anastasia. |
| JACK | I can't believe it. |
| TREVOR | You deserve it. |
| JACK | Cheers, Trevor. Pass on my thanks. It's really appreciated. |
| TREVOR | No problem. Anyway, I must fly. I've got a golfing date with the Glenmaddoch lot to see if we can get sponsorship again. Don't want to be drinking this shit forever. |

*He laughs and exits. Jack pours himself another drink and sits back. After a few moments, there's a knock at the door.*

JACK            Come in.

*Mr X enters.*

|       |                                          |
|-------|------------------------------------------|
|       | How did you get in?                      |
| MR X  | We need to talk.                         |
| JACK  | You agreed. Your organisation agreed. The problem has been solved. |
| MR X  | That is true and we're very... very happy with the outcome. However, other things have come to our attention. |
| JACK  | Get out.                                 |
| MR X  | I've been told to give you this.         |

*He searches in his satchel and pulls out an envelope.*

Oh sorry that's my electricity bill. Now where in goodness is... sorry about this. Ah... here we go.

*He hands him an envelope.*

| JACK  | What's this?                             |
|-------|------------------------------------------|
| MR X  | A list.                                  |
| JACK  | A list of what?                          |
| MR X  | Names. (*Pause*) It has come to our attention that your treasurer is a member |

of a pro-life organisation. We find this unacceptable. One of your male dancers supports Israel's war on Gaza. We find this unacceptable. Your new choreographer is the son of a top multi-nationalist who is involved in the illegal extraction of oil in the Niger Delta. This is unacceptable. Your accountant is a member of an orange lodge. Unacceptable.

*Jack begins to laugh.*

Your PR officer bought a real animal fur from Harrods last week. Again unacceptable. And your marketing assistant eats at McDonalds. Totally unacceptable.

*Jack continues laughing.*

**The End**